BRITAIN IN OLD PH(

BLACK COUNTRY RAILWAYS

N E D   W I L L I A M S

ALAN SUTTON PUBLISHING LIMITED

Alan Sutton Publishing Limited
Phoenix Mill · Far Thrupp · Stroud
Gloucestershire · GL5 2BU

First published 1995

Copyright © Ned Williams, 1995

*Cover photographs: front: 44840 passing
Tipton box on a Blackpool–New Street express,
c. 1960; back: local comedian Tommy Mundon
christening The Blackcountryman (31106) to
mark the twentieth anniversary of the founding
of the Black Country Society.*

British Library Cataloguing in Publication Data.
A catalogue record for this book is available from
the British Library.

ISBN 0-7509-0934-X

Typeset in 9/10 Sabon.
Typesetting and origination by
Alan Sutton Publishing Limited.
Printed in Great Britain by
Ebenezer Baylis, Worcester.

THE BLACK COUNTRY SOCIETY

This voluntary society, affiliated to the Civic Trust, was founded in 1967 as a reaction to the trend of the late 1950s and early 1960s to amalgamate everything into large units and in the Midlands to sweep away the area's industrial heritage in the process.

The general aim of the Society is to create interest in the past, present and future of the Black Country, and early on it campaigned for the establishment of an industrial museum. In 1975 the Black Country Museum was started by Dudley Borough Council on 26 acres of totally derelict land adjoining the grounds of Dudley Castle. This has developed into an award-winning museum which attracts over 250,000 visitors annually.

There are over two thousand members of the Black Country Society and all receive the quarterly magazine *The Blackcountryman*, of which over 112 issues have been published since its founding in 1967. In the whole collection there are some 1,700 authoritative articles on all aspects of the Black Country by historians, teachers, researchers, students, subject experts and ordinary folk with an extraordinary story to tell. The whole constitutes a unique resource about the area and is a mine of information for students and researchers who frequently refer to it. Many schools and libraries are subscribers. Three thousands copies of the magazine are printed each quarter. It is non-commercial, and contributors do not receive payment for their articles.

PO Box 71 · Kingswinford · West Midlands DY6 9YN

Contents

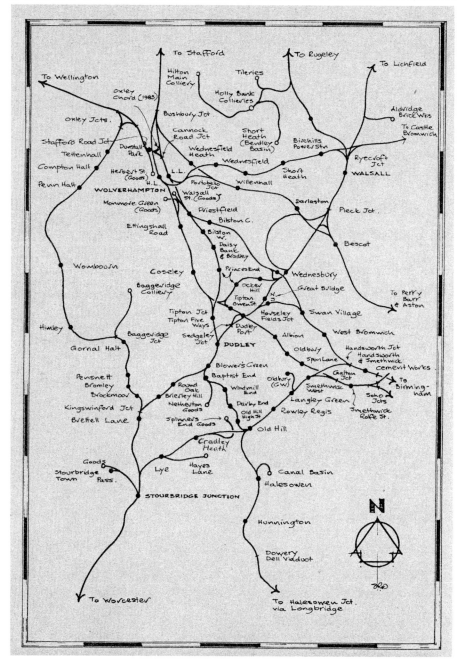

The railways of the Black Country.

Introduction

In the aftermath of the Second World War, there was an upsurge of interest in planning and social and political organization that many hoped would lead to the construction of a new and better world. In 1948 the West Midlands Group published their famous survey of Birmingham and the Black Country entitled *Conurbation*. It has become a classic of such regional surveys, but it is mentioned here because one of its many imaginative ways of presenting information to its readers was to ask them to imagine a trip across the region by train. In forty-eight 'snaps' taken through the carriage window on a rail journey from Birmingham New Street to Wolverhampton High Level, the reader is given an unparalleled visual transect of the Black Country: a montage of factories, canals, spoil banks, back yards, streets of terraced houses, chimneys and furnaces, and, above all, vast areas of dereliction and waste, in which the horizon is hidden by the industrial smog. Trees do not exist!

Nearly fifty years later, this journey is very different – and, in many respects, less interesting – but it is not just the view from the carriage window that has changed. What has also changed is that we would no longer think of trying to understand a region by taking a railway journey through it. What we do now is pile a few interesting buildings into a museum and visit them by travelling by road!

No doubt, every form of transport could be promoted as the best way of seeing a region. Imagine the Black Country as seen from the back of a horse, from the front upstairs seat of a bus, from the deck of a narrowboat or from the basket of a hot-air balloon, etc. However, this book invites you to look at the Black Country from the window of the railway carriage, and to look at the railways themselves as a way of understanding the region, and answering those never-ending questions: What is the relationship of one place to another? What is going on where? And why, in 1995, can you only travel from Wolverhampton to Walsall by rail by going via Birmingham?

Historically, the railways contributed to the development of the Black Country landscape after the canals had already created it, and before the roads had set about destroying it. In other words, the railways belonged to that Black Country that so many of us liked – the Black Country that embraced the Industrial Revolution and took on its own unique urban character, before motorways and the growth of suburbia conspired to make post-industrial provincial England look 'all the same'.

The first railway to be constructed in the Black Country was built to link a coalfield to the canal system. The most recent railway built in the Black Country was a monorail provided to link a car park to a shopping centre. The former opened in 1829, the latter in 1991. As I write this introduction, new railway stations are being built in the Black Country and some folk are itching to begin construction of the Midland Metro, so perhaps the story of a local rail transport is not yet over; but for the reasons outlined above, most of us think of the railways being an important part of the local scene perhaps for a mere hundred years – say from 1860 to 1960.

Before that time, roads and canals had been the transport systems that added to the shaping of the Black Country. Since that time, the motorways, and their feeders, have transformed the local landscape, altered our social habits and given us a sense of location. A 'furriner' looking for the Black Country is helped by knowing that it is where the M5 meets the M6; an American cinema magnate looking for a place to build a cinema chose Junction 10; the Development Corporation looking for the region's salvation chose to construct the Black Country Spine Road. No wonder that when we think of local railways, rightly or wrongly we think of the past!

Unlike the railways in other conurbations, the Black Country lines did not carry heavy commuter traffic. The only commuter traffic that has developed and been maintained is commuter traffic to Birmingham. The 'journey-to-work pattern' within the Black Country itself has always been a criss-cross of journeys, not journeys to a single centre, and many people have, until recently, lived fairly close to their work. That is why some lines lost their passenger services so long ago, and why the 'Beeching axe' could so easily be applied to large towns like Dudley.

In an important industrial area, one would expect that the railways played an important part in moving raw materials and finished goods, but again, things are not that simple in the Black Country. An analysis of the local use of the railway for the carrying of freight is beyond the scope of this book, but a casual glance at the photographs will reveal how little local freight traffic now uses the rails.

In the last three decades, the railway network of the Black Country has greatly contracted, but the surviving lines have been modernized, symbolized by the electrification of the main lines in 1967. Sectorization preceded the current moves towards privatization, but the story is not finished yet – by the time you read this book, trains will once again be running from the Black Country into Birmingham's new Snow Hill station and construction of the Metro should have begun. Who knows what might happen next?

This book takes the view that the past ended yesterday and that a photograph is 'old' if it shows something that cannot be photographed again today. The aim in selecting photographs has been to present diversity and, at the same time, to be as comprehensive as space permits. The Black Country was seldom the destination of railway photographers, and within the Black Country itself there are some lines that were considerably less photographed than others. Generally, we owe an enormous debt to local people, who did take the Black Country railways seriously enough to photograph them, and who have made their pictures available for books such as this. From the number of names credited, you will see that it is only possible to build up a comprehensive view of local railways by looking at the work of a large number of photographers – it is not a subject that has ever been encompassed by the work of an individual.

The message is simple: keep on taking photographs, keep on looking for 'old' photographs, keep on sharing what you have recorded and what you have found. Long may an interest in Black Country railways continue.

Section One

HISTORICAL OUTLINE

Every schoolchild once knew that Stephenson's *Rocket* won the Rainhill Trials on the Liverpool & Manchester Railway in 1829 – reinforcing the legend that railways were exclusively developed in Northern England. In the Black Country, a railway was planned in 1827, and two years later, in the year of the Rainhill Trials, a railway was opened from Shut End, near Pensnett, to Ashwood on the Staffordshire & Worcestershire Canal. *Agenoria* was built in Stourbridge to the designs of the railway's engineer, John Urpeth Raistrick, and on 2 June 1829, a huge crowd turned out to see her pull the first 'passenger train' in the Black Country. Eight trucks carried 360 passengers, and a further four trucks carried 3½ tons of coal on the 2 mile journey. On a third run, the locomotive reached the speed of 11 m.p.h.

After all this excitement, the railway, a joint venture by the Earl of Dudley and James Foster, settled down to a workaday life of carrying coal to the canal and serving the Shut End Works – an integrated complex of pits, blast furnaces and ironworks that began to develop after the opening of the railway. Eventually, this pioneering railway became just a part of the huge system built by the Earl of Dudley, usually known as the Pensnett Railway. *Agenoria* retired and was presented to the Science Museum at South Kensington in 1885.

The real railway invasion of the Black Country began in the mid-1830s, represented by the opening of the Grand Junction Railway in July 1837. On its way from Birmingham to the Mersey, the Grand Junction line skirted the Black Country and bypassed principal towns. Of greater local significance was the Oxford, Worcester & Wolverhampton Railway, which was authorized in 1845, and further lines authorized in 1846 and opened in the 1850s: the Shrewsbury & Birmingham Railway and the South Staffordshire line, which proposed to link Dudley with Walsall and beyond. Further lines opened in the 1850s: the Birmingham, Wolverhampton & Stour Valley Railway – whose achievement was to build the 'main line' from Birmingham to Wolverhampton rather than to serve the 'Stour Valley' mentioned in its title – and the Birmingham Wolverhampton & Dudley Railway, which was to provide the Great Western Railway with a way of extending its broad gauge north of Birmingham and into the Black Country.

As the smaller, 'local' companies were amalgamated and absorbed into larger concerns, the Black Country emerged as a frontier and battleground between two major companies: the Great Western Railway and the London & North Western Railway. The Midland Railway made one foray into the Black Country by acquiring the Wolverhampton & Walsall Railway (opened 1872) from the LNWR in 1876. The second half of the nineteenth century saw the systems extended, with a number of interconnecting lines and a few branches, and a gradual upgrading of the lines that gave them their distinctive company appearance in everything from rolling stock to station buildings. The area was served both by local trains and by long-distance trains; the latter consisted of services that passed through the Black Country and services that terminated in the region, particularly at Wolverhampton.

The company rivalries continued after the Railway Amalgamations of 1923, and the Black Country found itself hosting the GWR and the LMS (the London Midland & Scottish Railway). Even after nationalization in 1948, the area was served by two regions until everything was brought into the London Midland Region on 1 January 1963.

The *Agenoria*, built at Stourbridge under the supervision of Mr Rastrick, and presented to the public at the opening of the Shut End Railway on 2 June 1829. This picture of the locomotive is thought to date from about 1870. (Collection of the late W.V.K. Gale.)

Alma was built by E.B. Wilson in 1856 (works no. 548) for the Earl of Dudley's Pensnett Railway, then still physically separated from the Shut End Railway. The first tracks of the Pensnett Railway were laid in 1844, and over the years it underwent considerable expansion, centred from the mid-1850s onwards on the earl's ironworks at Round Oak. In the early 1860s, the line was extended to pits in the earl's Himley Coalfield, and it is here that *Alma* was photographed. (Collection of the late W.V.K. Gale.)

Brandon (Manning Wardle no. 6 of 1859) was one of two further locomotives provided for the expanding Pensnett Railway (the other was *Himley*). It is seen here in the 1870s or 1880s at Kingswinford, where the Shut End Railway and Pensnett Railway were united in 1865. (Collection of the late W.V.K. Gale.)

While the Earl of Dudley and James Foster were building and developing their private railway on the west of the Black Country, the Grand Junction Railway was bringing the first public railway to the eastern fringe of the region. This Victorian print shows us Newton Road station – one of the original intermediate stations on the 1837 line. (Collection of the late W.V.K. Gale.)

In more recent times, Newton Road station simply consisted of a level-crossing and standard LNWR signal-box. (Nigel Hazlewood.)

Newton station, crossing and signal-box on a site slightly south of the original station, 1900s. The hamlet of Newton lost its railway station altogether in 1945. In the GJR's scheme of things, it served the distant town of West Bromwich. (Collection of Letitia Harris.)

The standard gauge (of the Oxford, Worcester & Wolverhampton Railway) and the broad gauge (of the Great Western Railway) met at Priestfield, and mixed gauge tracks enabled trains to reach and share Wolverhampton Low Level station by the end of 1854. This view of the mixed gauge trackwork, *c.* 1870, looks southwards through the Wednesfield Road Bridge towards the train shed of the joint station. The GWR withdrew broad gauge trains from the Black Country in 1869. (Collection of Eric Hamilton.)

No. 3231, a 2–4–0 of the 3226 class, stands just south of the Sun Street Bridge at Wolverhampton Low Level station, *c.* 1912. The Shrewsbury & Birmingham Railway became part of the GWR in 1854. The Oxford, Worcester & Wolverhampton Railway became part of the West Midland Railway in July 1860, which, in turn, became part of the GWR in August 1863. Thus two main lines serving the Black Country, and converging at Wolverhampton firmly became part of the GWR, and Wolverhampton established itself on the company's hierarchy of 'important places'. (Collection of Roger Carpenter.)

The GWR broad gauge reached its northern extremity at Stafford Road Engine Shed, seen at the far left of this picture, taken in the late 1880s when the broad gauge rails had vanished from the scene. The Shrewsbury & Birmingham Railway had opened a shed and repairs facility near this site towards the end of 1849. After the S&BR/GWR merger of 1854, the Stafford Road area developed both as a shed and works. Locomotives were built at Stafford Road Works from 1859 until 1908, but the site went through further transformations to provide repair facilities until 1964. (Collection of Eric Hamilton.)

The GWR's broad gauge heritage is still apparent in this turn-of-the-century view of Wednesbury station. The space between the platforms had once accommodated mixed gauge tracks. The 'Dean Single' locomotive on the Up train entering the station has just passed the Patent Shaft Steelworks. (Photograph taken by Dr Dingley, a well-known amateur photographer in Wednesbury, and copied in the 1950s by C.J. Selway.)

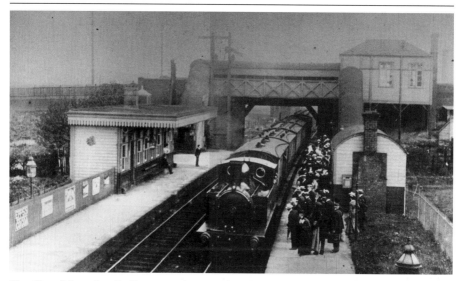

The Grand Junction Railway amalgamated with other railways on 1 January 1846 to form the London & North Western Railway (LNWR). By the 1880s, such lines had taken on a fairly standardized LNWR appearance, well represented by the train and various buildings seen here in this view of Darlaston station about the turn of the century, where the 0–6–2T brings its train of 'plum and spilt milk' six-wheelers into the crowded Down (Wolverhampton-bound) platform. (Collection of Darlaston Local History Society.)

The LNWR style is well represented by this picture of 2–4–0 no. 2064, *Autocrat*, at Walsall station, just after the turn of the century. This station was used by LNWR and Midland Railway trains, but was of general LNWR appearance, with some added interest provided by the original South Staffordshire Railway's buildings alongside Station Street. (Collection of Roger Carpenter.)

In 1923, the railways of Great Britain were 'amalgamated' or 'grouped' into four large companies. Until then, the façade of Wolverhampton High Level station had carried three large signs to greet passengers. Midland and LNWR passengers proceeded straight ahead into the booking office of the High Level station, and GWR passengers headed to the left to descend, via a subway, to the Low Level station beyond. After 1923, the signs were reduced to two, and in this view, taken in 1933, the London, Midland & Scottish Railway (LMS) sign is clearly visible. (Collection of Eric Hamilton.)

Modern LMS locomotives and passenger stock eventually appeared on Black Country main lines, but the local services and the infrastructure continued to have a very 'pre-grouping' look about them. Here, as late as August 1947, LMS 2–4–2T no. 6704 pauses at Darlaston while propelling its train from Wolverhampton to Walsall. The locomotive and station, and distant signal-box, are all pure LNWR. Enamel signs for Stephens Ink and Calverts Disinfectant can be found on the station fence between adverts for Brylcreem and a timetable board for the Great Northern Railway of Ireland. (W.A. Camwell.)

The Great Western Railway was even less affected by the 1923 'Grouping' – even retaining its pre-grouping name. When this picture was taken, in 1925, Wolverhampton Low Level station still retained its all-over roof. During the 1920s and into the 1930s, the GWR improved and modernized some of its facilities in Wolverhampton and the Black Country. In 1927, the GWR introduced its fine new express passenger locomotives – the 'King' class – and these worked the London trains from Low Level. Here a much more humble locomotive, 2–6–2T no. 4528, stands at Low Level. (Collection of Roger Carpenter.)

GWR 'Hall' class 4–6–0 no. 4974, *Brangwyn Hall*, stands at Wolverhampton Low Level station, 1947 – just before nationalization. Note that the all-over roof has been removed, and the station has a much more 'open' quality, which survived for the rest of its life. The all-over roof at High Level remained until the 1960s, and therefore post-war photographers generally made for the Low Level. In a town like Wolverhampton, company loyalties could be strong and competition was intense, but few could have imagined that the GWR line would fade away and the LMS would become the modern railway. (Roy Smith.)

Modernization, dieselization, electrification and rationalization have all affected the changing face of local railways from the 1950s through to the present day. The early LMR diesels, 10000 and 10001, and even the SR 10202, were all seen traversing the Black Country in the 1950s. In 1960, the WR introduced the 'Birmingham Pullman', a diesel train, which left Wolverhampton Low Level station every morning at 7.00 a.m. Here it is seen at the Low Level station upon its return at the end of the day. Its striking blue livery was a contrast to the green of the diesel multiple unit seen on the right in the Shrewsbury bay. (Eric Hamilton.)

The LMR main line through the Black Country, still known as the Stour Valley Line, was chosen for modernization and electrification in the 1960s, in effect leading to the eclipse and demise of the Western Region lines. The electric trains began running in 1967, by which time stations had been closed or modernized and signal-boxes had closed as the line came under the control of power boxes at Wolverhampton and Birmingham. A survivor has been the 'ARP' box at Watery Lane, Tipton (built with a concrete roof as an air-raid precaution in 1939). The box and old-fashioned gates contrast with this class 86 electric locomotive no. 86102 and its train passing through the Black Country, 24 July 1985. (Ned Williams.)

Much of the Black Country rail network has now disappeared. This picture was taken on 6 March 1972 at Wednesbury Central, on the last day of operation of the GWR main line that traversed the Black Country on its way from Birmingham Snow Hill to Wolverhampton Low Level station. Wednesbury Town on the Dudley–Walsall line had already closed to passengers in 1964. (Roger Crombleholme.)

This photograph was taken from the parapet of the former GWR bridge at Wednesbury and looks down on the Walsall–Dudley line on 19 March 1993, as the train crosses Potters Lane on its way to Brierley Hill. Class 47 diesel locomotive no. 47238, christened *Bescot Yard* at a local ceremony in October 1988, carries special headboards, 'The Pensnett Knocker' and 'The Dudley Dasher Memorial Special', to mark the closure on that day of the line between Bescot and Round Oak. The route, made up of former LMS and GWR lines on either side of Dudley, made a fascinating transect of the Black Country. (Ned Williams.)

Section Two

THE EX-GWR MAIN LINES

The Black Country was served by two GWR main lines that met just south of Wolverhampton. The best-known was the line from Birmingham Snow Hill that came out through Winson Green and Hockley and entered the Black Country by crossing the boundary of Staffordshire near Handsworth & Smethwick station. It proceeded, via Hawthorns Halt, close to the Albion FC ground, to West Bromwich, then to Swan Village in the heart of the Black Country. North of Swan Village the line passed through Hill Top Tunnel and descended to Wednesbury, and on to Bilston. It joined the 'other' main line at Priestfield and made its way to Wolverhampton Low Level station, continuing north to make connections with the Shrewsbury line and to join the LMS near Bushbury.

This line had been planned as the Birmingham, Wolverhampton & Dudley Railway and was incorporated in August 1846, just before parliament took steps to enforce the construction of standard gauge railways. It was vested into the GWR two years later. It was built to extend the GWR's broad gauge empire north-westwards, from Oxford up to Birmingham and across the Black Country, with the eventual aim of reaching the Mersey. The line across the Black Country was laid with mixed gauge track, and the northernmost point a broad gauge locomotive could reach was Stafford Road Junction, just north of Wolverhampton. The line opened on 14 November 1854. Mixed gauge track only remained in use until the end of March 1869, and no photographs seem to have survived to record broad gauge trains in the Black Country.

Eventually, this GWR main line through the Black Country was host to express passenger services running between London Paddington and Birkenhead, and Wolverhampton became the intermediate stop where engines were changed. Other express services linked Wolverhampton to a number of destinations, but these trains, by their very nature, did not stop at any of the other Black Country stations on the line. The stations at Bilston, Swan Village, West Bromwich, etc. (and the short-lived station at Bradley & Moxley, opened June 1860) were served by local trains.

The GWR and LNWR (later LMS) obviously competed for London–Wolverhampton traffic, and the GWR was rather handicapped by having the longer route. The ex-GWR line eventually enjoyed a heyday in the 1960s, while the other line was being electrified, but once this was completed in 1967, the GWR line went into decline. The local trains were soon reduced to a few shuttle services between Snow Hill and Wolverhampton Low Level station and these were finally withdrawn in March 1972. Short pieces of the former main line were retained for specialized goods traffic into the 1980s, and the last piece of track on the old main line lasted until 1992 – a single, rusty spur from Wednesbury to Norton's Siding by Loxdale Road, Bilston. A final twist in the fortunes of the line is that the section from Handsworth Junction into Snow Hill re-opens in 1995, with a brand new Black Country station at The Hawthorns, and there is still a possibility that the Midland Metro might be built along much of the ex-GWR trackbed.

A Western Region express passes through the Black Country, 12 September 1958. Ex-GWR 'Grange' class 4–6–0 no. 6862, *Derwent Grange*, brings the 5.20 p.m. train from Wolverhampton Low Level station to Paddington alongside the Up platform at West Bromwich. The large, square, classical building on the Up platform was typical of the buildings provided on this line, but the waiting room on the left was a recent addition! (Michael Mensing.)

'Black Five' 4–6–0 no. 44884 approaches Wolverhampton Low Level station from the north as class 4 2–6–0 no. 76038 departs, *c*. 1965. Note the High Level line in the background. (Brian Robbins.)

The two GWR main lines through the Black Country converged at Wolverhampton Low Level station, and therefore we begin our survey at this station. Trainspotters and a photographer record the scene at the southern end of Low Level on 7 August 1965. 'Hall' class 4–6–0 no. 6991, *Acton Burnall Hall*, waits to take over the Up train from 'Black Five' 4–6–0 no. 44679. (Eric Hamilton.)

The view from the Wolverhampton–Bilston road bridge reveals ex-GWR 'King' class 4–6–0 no. 6006, *King George I*, accelerating past Monmore Green Stadium with a Birkenhead–Paddington express, *c.* 1960. The tracks on the left provided access to the Walsall Street goods yard, and the rear of the train is passing Stow Heath signal-box. (Barry Price.)

At Priestfield, the main line to Birmingham curves away sharply from its junction with the West Midland line, and 'Black Five' 4–6–0 no. 44808 brings a freight train, tender first, past the Up platform, 20 April 1966. (Ralph Amos.)

Ex-GWR 2–6–2T no. 5192 enters Bilston Central station with a Wolverhampton–Birmingham local train in June 1957, while the new waiting room on the Down platform was being built. (Collection of Roger Carpenter.)

A DMU (Diesel Multiple Unit) for Wolverhampton leaves the Down platform, with its new shelter, at Bilston Central station, as an ex-GWR 0–6–0PT travels as a light engine past the new awning on the main building on the Up platform, *c.* 1960. (Peter Shoesmith.)

Ex-GWR 'Castle' class 4–6–0 no. 7032, *Denbigh Castle*, on the 1.10 p.m. Paddington–Wolverhampton train passes Norton's Siding, just south of Bilston, Sunday 30 July 1961. Compare this view with the one at the foot of page 108. (Michael Mensing.)

Ex-GWR 47xx class 2–8–0 no. 4708 enters Wednesbury Central from the south, early 1960s. The rear of the train has just crossed the bridge carrying the GWR main line over the South Staffordshire line from Walsall to Dudley. (David Wilson.)

A GWR 'Dean Single' passes through Wednesbury at the turn of the century with a southbound Up express. BR added 'Central' to the station names at Wednesbury and Bilston in 1950 to distinguish them from other stations serving the same town. (Collection of Roger Carpenter.)

Ex-GWR 0–6–0PT no. 8739 and 'Hall' class 4–6–0 no. 6994, *Baggrave Hall*, await their fate at Wednesbury Exchange Sidings, with the station building at Wednesbury Central seen clearly in the background, 14 February 1965. (Eric Hamilton.)

Ex-GWR 0–6–0PT no. 3792 emerges from the southern portal of Hill Top Tunnel and begins the descent to Swan Village, 20 August 1965. (Ralph Amos.)

A class 15xx 0–6–0PT, built after nationalization to Hawksworth's design, pauses just north of Swan Village, *c.* 1960. Behind the train is a large goods yard, provided in the 1920s, to deal with coal delivery. The engine's condition suggests that it has just been overhauled at Stafford Road Works. (David Wilson.)

'Britannia' class 4–6–2 no. 70053, *Moray Firth*, with its reporting number chalked on the smokebox door, storms through Swan Village, *c*. 1964. The new brick station buildings lacked the elegance of their wooden predecessors. The building on the left stretched across to the platform serving the Dudley line, which closed at the end of June 1964. (David Owen.)

A picture taken from the same bridge on 3 August 1957 shows the wooden structures that once graced Swan Village, and ex-GWR 'Grange' class 4–6–0 no. 6866, *Morfa Grange*, arriving with a 'semi-fast' Up train. Hill Top provides the distant horizon to this picture. (Michael Mensing.)

Swan Village gas holder forms the backdrop to this view of ex-GWR 2–6–2T no. 4165, climbing towards West Bromwich with its train of coal wagons, 6 September 1962. (Ralph Amos.)

Ex-GWR 'King' class 4–6–0 no. 6001, *King George V*, comes through West Bromwich with an express for Paddington, *c.* 1960. (Eric Rogers.)

Ex-GWR 'County' class 4–6–0 no. 1026 *County of Salop* passes Handsworth Junction and comes through Hawthorns Halt with a Bournemouth–Birkenhead train, 25 March 1961. The lines curving out of the right-hand side of the picture are the 'Stourbridge Extension' – which has come back into use on 24 September 1995, as trains once again run from the Extension line, through a new Hawthorns station to Snow Hill. (Michael Mensing.)

The southernmost station on the GWR main line that could be regarded as lying in the Black Country would have been Handsworth & Smethwick. Ex-GWR 2–6–2T no. 6128 is seen leaving with a stopping train to Wolverhampton, 3 February 1962. (Ron Moss.)

The other GWR main line traversing the Black Country left the Wolverhampton–Birmingham line at Priestfield (see foot of page 22) and was often known as the 'West Midland' line. Ex-GWR 'Grange' class 4–6–0 no. 6828, *Trellech Grange*, draws into the West Midland platform at Priestfield with a stopping train to Worcester, 1 June 1957. (Roger Carpenter.)

Bilston West, Bradley & Daisy Bank, Coseley and Tipton Five Ways were not very frequently photographed stations, perhaps because the train service ceased in the summer of 1962, just before photographers had awoken to the need to record such lines. Here a 'Prairie' drifts into Bradley & Daisy Bank at the end of the 1950s. (Phil Lycett.)

Ex-GWR 'Castle' class 4–6–0, no. *5098*, *Clifford Castle*, runs into Dudley from the West Midland line on a Fridays-only light engine movement to Stourbridge Junction, *c.* 1962. Note Dudley East signal-box on the right and the South Staffordshire line passing under Tipton Road. (George Bennett.)

GWR 'Hall' class 4–6–0 no. 6901, *Arley Hall*, pauses at the West Midland line platform at Dudley on a train to Worcester, 1948. Note the locomotive has not yet been given the 'BR' treatment, and the station is still in wartime 'grime'. (Roy Smith.)

Dudley station lost its passenger services one by one between 1962 and 1964, and was demolished early in 1967 to make way for the new Freightliner Depot, which opened on 6 November 1967 and closed on 29 September 1986. The line occupied in this picture by class 45 no. 45003 and the train of china clay empties, on 9 May 1965, eventually closed in March 1993. (Peter Green.)

Looking south from Dudley station, we see diesel cars, no. W55004 and no. 55002, which have come up from Old Hill to form the 16.30 p.m. service back to Old Hill, 4 July 1962. In the background is Kates Hill, through which the railway had to tunnel to reach the south-western quadrant of the Black Country. (Graham Sidwell.)

The first station south of Dudley was Blowers Green, and here a grimy, unidentified 'Castle' calls at Blowers Green on its way to Worcester, 1948. Note the Palethorpes' Sausages van on the train going northwards and Dudley Gas Works on the skyline. (Roy Smith.)

Blowers Green Junction, with the 'Bumble Hole' line to Old Hill curving away to the right in the foreground and ex-GWR 'Hall' class 4–6–0 no. 6927, *Lilford Hall*, passing the signal-box on the West Midland line with the Tavistock–Crewe goods train, 10 August 1965. (Richard Taylor.)

Just south of Blowers Green, the GWR crossed a valley full of canals, via the Parkhead Viaduct. The canals were drained on 10 March 1993, when class 37s no. 37040 and no. 37077 traversed the viaduct with the Bescot–Cardiff train, but the area has recently been landscaped and the canals restored. The track across the viaduct has now been lifted, and this landmark now awaits its fate. (Paul Dorney.)

As the West Midland line approached Brierley Hill, one of its most famous features was the level-crossing at Round Oak with the Earl of Dudley's Railway. Local legend stated that the Earl's trains had priority, as his railway was there first! Andrew Barclay 0–6–0ST, *Duchess of Gloucester* (no. 2110 of 1941) crosses the main line, *c.* 1960. (Collection of Keith Gale.)

Kingswinford Junction, as class 47 no. 47200 backs wagons into Moor Street Yard, 21 March 1986. The West Midland line makes its way from right to left diagonally across the picture, and the branch to Pensnett, Wombourn and Oxley can be seen behind the first two wagons of the train. (Brian Robbins.)

An unidentified 'Grange' class locomotive climbs through Brettell Lane station with a goods train that will take the Wombourn line at Kingswinford Junction, 8 February 1964. Heavy trains could require assistance between Stourbridge Junction and Dudley. Note the parcels traffic on the platform. (David Wilson.)

The West Midland line crossed the valley of the River Stour on the Stambermill Viaduct, seen here about 1960. The brick viaduct seen here was built by the GWR in the 1880s to replace the early timber viaduct provided by the Oxford, Worcester & Wolverhampton Railway when the line opened in the 1850s. (John Dew.)

Ex-GWR 'County' class 4–6–0 no. 1016, *County of Hants*, leaves the southern end of Stourbridge Junction station with a Worcester train, *c.* 1960. At Stourbridge Junction, the West Midland line met the 'Stourbridge Extension' line which served Lye, Cradley Heath, Old Hill, etc., on its way to Birmingham. This signal-box was closed in 1973. (John Dew.)

THE EX-LNWR
MAIN LINES

The first main line to venture close to the Black Country was the Grand Junction Railway, opened on 4 July 1837, from Birmingham to Warrington. It entered the Black Country at Newton Road and first provided stations at Bescot Bridge (for Walsall), James Bridge (Darlaston), Willenhall, and 'Wolverhampton' (put in inverted commas as the station was at Wednesfield Heath). These stations changed their names and geographical location over the years, partly as a rationalization process, and partly because towns like Walsall and Wolverhampton were eventually served by stations closer to their centres. A month after the Stour Valley line was opened in 1852 (see below), a station was provided at Bushbury, where the two lines met.

The Grand Junction line grazed the north-eastern and eastern fringes of the Black Country and was more concerned with its place in the growing national network – railways stretching from the Thames to the Mersey – than with its local significance to the Black Country. Ironically, this function was later better served by the even more direct Trent Valley line, well to the east of the Black Country. Locally the GJ route became known as 'The Old Line' with the opening of the Stour Valley line, and the very name indicates the way in which it has been consigned to obscurity, although important enough to figure in the grand electrification of the railways from London to the north-west in the 1960s. This relative obscurity is the reason why this line has not been frequently photographed.

The direct line from Birmingham to Wolverhampton through the heart of the Black Country is known as the 'Stour Valley', as it was incorporated on 3 August 1846 as the Birmingham, Wolverhampton & Stour Valley Railway. The latter part of the company's title referred to the intention of building a line from somewhere near Smethwick to the valley of the River Stour, and thence to Stourbridge and Stourport.

A quarter stake in the scheme was held by the Shrewsbury & Birmingham Railway, who hoped that it would provide the link they needed from Wolverhampton to Birmingham. In all other respects, the scheme fell into the camp of the London & North Western Railway, which had been formed at the beginning of 1846 by the amalgamation of the Grand Junction Railway and the London & Birmingham Railway.

This was logical, as the Stour Valley line was to leave the LNWR at Bushbury and join it again in Birmingham.

It was not completed without some delays and the infamous battles with the Shrewsbury & Birmingham Railway at Wolverhampton, but on 1 July 1852, trains began to run, and the Black Country was served by new stations at Smethwick, Spon Lane, Oldbury & Bromford Lane, Dudley Port, Tipton, Deepfields (known as 'Deepfields & Coseley' two years later), Ettingshall & Bilston Road and Wolverhampton Queen Street (known as 'High Level' from 1885 onwards).

The Stour Valley line was used in the West Midland Group's *Conurbation* to provide a series of 'snaps' of the Black Country. Today, the immediate lineside has been 'greened', and the landscape on the other side of the railway fence has changed beyond recognition – but it is still our principal main line, traversed by expresses from the Black Country to the capital, and by trains running to and from all the corners of the realm.

Ex-LMS 'Jubilee' class 4–6–0 no. 45670, *Howard of Effingham*, brings a Whit Sunday excursion off the Stour Valley line, 17 May 1964. Looking south towards Wolverhampton from the Bushbury Lane bridge, it is possible to see the junction of the Grand Junction and Stour Valley lines, although it is difficult to imagine the Bushbury station that was open here from 1 July 1852 until 1 May 1912. Note the posts being erected for electrification of these lines. (Michael Mensing.)

The Stour Valley line climbs all the way to Wolverhampton High Level station. Ex-LMS 'Coronation' class 4–6–0 no. 462240, *City of Coventry*, brings empty stock into High Level station to form the 16.20 to Euston, *c.* 1960. (Ralph Amos.)

Ex-LMS 'Black Five' 4–6–0 no. 44748 draws into the Up platform at Wolverhampton High Level station, as seen from the footbridge beneath the all-over roof, *c.* 1960. (Michael Paine.)

Looking north towards High Level station just after the all-over roof had been removed and while the track layout was being altered pending electrification, 15 August 1964. On the left is the Mill Street goods shed, and in the background is Jones' Mill. Wolverhampton's LNWR heritage is celebrated by the survival of ex-LNWR 0–8–0 no. 48895 into the era of the Beatles. (Peter Hale.)

South of Wolverhampton, *c.* 1962. The Stour Valley line can be seen curving to the right, as ex-LMS 'Black Five' 4–6–0 no. 44714 brings a train off the connecting line that links High Level station to the GJ line at Portobello Junction, opened in 1881. (Peter Hale.)

Apart from a short-lived station at Monmore Green, the first station south of Wolverhampton on the Stour Valley line was Ettingshall Road & Bilston; even this station closed in 1964. The wooden buildings on the Up platform are shown here as passengers wait for a train – just before closure. (David Smith.)

Ettingshall Road station originally had a brick-built building, which can be seen on the left of this picture, in about 1930, looking into the goods yard at the famous 'Ketcham's Corner', now the site of an office block. (Author's collection.)

An unidentified ex-LMS 'Black Five' 4–6–0 with a mixed freight train at Spring Vale in the late 1950s. Behind the train is Stewart & Lloyds Bilston Steelworks, and in the foreground is the Birmingham Canal Navigation, then still in commercial use. (Barry Price.)

Class 50 no. 50025, in Network Southeast livery, approaches Spring Vale from the south with a Saturdays-only service to Wolverhampton from Paddington, 22 July 1989. This picture was taken from the new bridge just opened to carry the Black Country Link Road across railway and canal. (Ned Williams.)

Steaming through Coseley: ex-LMS 'Jubilee' class 4–6–0 no. 45593, *Kolhapur*, heads an excursion to Blackpool, Sunday 30 July 1961. (Michael Mensing.)

Ex-LMS 'Jubilee' class no. 45670, *Howard of Effingham*, passes Bloomfield Junction signal-box with an express to Birmingham New Street, *c.* 1962. Note the canal basin on the right and the wagon works, then reached from the West Midland line. (Lawrence Brownhill.)

Looking south from Bloomfield Junction signal-box, *c.* 1962. 'Black Five' 4–6–0 no. 45222 can be seen as it is about to disappear beneath the bridge carrying the West Midland line over the Stour Valley line. (Lawrence Brownhill.)

An unidentified ex-LMS 'Coronation' class locomotive glides through Tipton (Owen Street) station with an express, *c.* 1960. This was the signalman's view of the level-crossing and station. (Lawrence Brownhill.)

Just south of Tipton was Watery Lane Crossing signal-box, poised between railway and canal (see foot of page 17). Here, a Craven parcels car heads past the two gas works and makes for Dudley Port, which can just be seen on the skyline, Sunday 30 June 1961. (Michael Mensing.)

An ex-LMS class 6 Stanier 2–6–0 makes its way southwards alongside the canal between the two gas works at Tipton, the one on the left producing town gas, the one on the right producing Mond gas for industry, c. 1960. (David Wilson.)

An ex-LMS 'Black Five' no. 44939 leaves Dudley Port behind, 1962. Palethorpes' Sausages vans often awaited collection in the sidings in the foreground. (David Wilson.)

Another ex-LMS 'Black Five', but with Fowler tender, cruises past Albion station and signal-box with a train of coaches in the early BR carmine-and-cream livery, 1950s. (Eric Rogers.)

Ex-LMS 'Jubilee' class no. 45645, *Collingwood*, approaches Albion station from the Oldbury direction, 1963. The stretch of line from Dudley Port to Smethwick, through a very industrial landscape, was seldom photographed. (David Wilson.)

Spon Lane station on the day it closed to passenger traffic, 15 June 1964 – but Albion had closed four years earlier. Oldbury & Bromford Lane station fared better. It became simply 'Oldbury' in 1964, and then disappeared to be reborn as 'Sandwell & Dudley' on 14 May 1984. (Joe Russell.)

Class 87 no. 87005, *City of London*, streaks through Galton valley at Smethwick, with the GWR bridge and Telford's Galton Bridge in the background, 8 May 1984. (Brian Robbins.)

The Galton Bridge forms the background to this view of a class 47 no. 47376 bringing the Handsworth cement train across the bridge over the Stour Valley line's electrified tracks in Smethwick, 19 May 1984. This is the location of the new Galton Junction station – opened 24 September 1995 – where interchange can take place between Stour Valley services and Stourbridge Junction–Snow Hill services. (Ned Williams.)

The Black Country's less well-known ex-LNWR main line is the Grand Junction line, which we traverse by travelling south once more, from Bushbury Junction. Ex-LMS 'Patriot' class 4–6–0 no. 45536, 'Private W. Wood V.C.', pulls away from Bushbury Junction with an Up express, 1950s. (John Davenport.)

The Grand Junction line skirted to the east of Wolverhampton across Wednesfield Heath, emerging here from the short tunnel beneath the Wyrley & Essington Canal and the Midland Railway's line into Wolverhampton. Class 85, no. 85035, heads an Up freight train, 4 May 1978. (Michael Mensing.)

A two-car DMU leaves Willenhall bound for Wolverhampton, 2 August 1963. The GJR stations at Willenhall and Darlaston survived to be served by local stopping trains until 18 January 1965, despite a few name changes (see page 14 top and 15 bottom). (Peter Shoesmith.)

An aerial view of Darlaston station and industrialized environs, 1950s. The sidings behind Martin Winn's nut and bolt factory are on the line from Darlaston Junction to Wednesbury, opened on 14 September 1863, and used by passenger trains until 1887 – probably the least-photographed stretch of railway in the Black Country! (Author's collection.)

Darlaston Junction in more recent times: class 31 no. 31203 stands on the Grand Junction line from Bescot. The 'Pleck Loop' (opened 1 March 1881) can be seen curving away to the right, on its way to Walsall, 17 June 1985. A decade later, locomotives are no longer seen in 'rail blue', and F.H. Lloyds steelworks have disappeared from the face of the earth. (Ned Williams.)

Two class 4F 0–6–0s, no. 44210 and no. 44155, head for Darlaston from Bescot, having passed under the South Staffordshire line which crosses the back of the picture, 2 August 1965. The Parthenon-like structure is part of the M6 motorway, which now totally obliterates this view. (Ralph Amos.)

Ex-LMS 'Coronation' class 4–6–2 no. 462228, *Duchess of Rutland*, on the Grand Junction by the banks of the Tame (the South Staffordshire line bridge is in the far background). Until the early 1960s, a 'Coronation' class was often to be seen passing through Bescot with an express about midday. (David Wilson.)

Ex-LMS 'Jubilee' class 4–6–0 no. 45593, *Kolhapur*, just north of Bescot, 1964. Note the siding into Elwell's works, and St Paul's Church on the Wednesbury skyline. New culverts for the Tame anticipate the building of the M6 where the photographer is standing. (David Owen.)

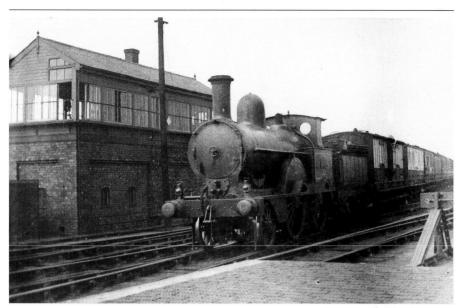

Contrasts at Bescot: a LNWR 'Precedent' class 2–4–0 no. 2178, *Pluck*, comes into Bescot station with a Down express, *c.* 1904. (Collection of Roger Carpenter.)

Bescot Open Day, 30 August 1992. BR class 8P 4–6–2 no. 71000, *Duke of Gloucester*, passes Bescot Traction Maintenance Depot with the 'Bescot Century Limited' – a rather grand name for a shuttle service provided within the yard! (Ned Williams.)

The ubiquitous *Howard of Effingham* ('Jubilee' class 4–6–0 no. 45670) pauses at Bescot, *c.* 1960. Like most ex-GJR stations, Bescot went through various changes of name and exact location, and these station buildings were demolished in 1967 to make way for the current minimal station, served by the Birmingham–Walsall electrified local trains. (Eric Rogers.)

It is already history that Centro, the transport authority in the West Midlands, has opened several new railway stations. The Grand Junction line leaves the Black Country as it passes through the new station at Tame Bridge – opened on 4 June 1990, and seen here one month later – a location enhanced by the canal aqueduct that crosses the line at this point. (Ned Williams.)

Section Four

BYWAYS

If the Black Country railway map consisted of only the four main lines illustrated in this book, all would be simple. The Black Country railway map is complex because of all the minor lines, branches and byways that have been added to the network over the years – and then been subtracted or modified. This section sets out to show the bewildering number and variety of such byways.

We begin by looking at the South Staffordshire line – built by the South Staffordshire Railway and absorbed into the LNWR and thus the LMS and the London Midland Region of BR. This line made a wonderful transect of the Black Country from east to west: from Walsall to Dudley. We also look at the Princes End Loop that left the South Staffordshire line at Wednesbury and ran to the Stour Valley line near Tipton. Although part of the GWR network, we then look at the Swan Village–Horseley Fields line, because at the latter point, the line joined the South Staffordshire line. The 'Stourbridge Extension' line made its way from west to east across the southern edge of the Black Country, running from the West Midlands line at Stourbridge Junction to the GWR Wolverhampton–Birmingham main line at Handsworth Junction, by The Hawthorns. This busy line also spawned branches, such as the Oldbury Branch from Langley Green, and the two lines radiating from Old Hill: the 'Bumble Hole Line' to Dudley and the line down to Halesowen.

We then transfer our attention to the western borderlands of the Black Country, where the line from Kingswinford Junction, on the West Midland line, made its way to Oxley, near Wolverhampton, via Wombourn. The line consisted of two distinct sections – the southernmost section serving an industrial area, and the northernmost section seeming quite rural. Having found ourselves in Wolverhampton, we pause to look at a couple of obscure but interesting lines – both of which have played their part in re-shaping the local railway map. We finish this section by looking at the Midland Railway's one venture into the Black Country, via their line from North Walsall to Wolverhampton.

In an area like the Black Country, byways often spawned further branches. Some, like the Netherton Goods Branch and the Halesowen Basin Branch, can be illustrated. Others, such as the Hayes Branch or the Spinners End Branch, seem to have been so 'obscure' that photographs of them do not seem to have come to light. Similarly, no one seems to have seen pictures of the passenger trains on the Wolverhampton–North Walsall line (withdrawn 1931), or a good, general view of life at Oldbury Basin, let alone a passenger train at Oldbury, last seen in March 1915.

A class 25 locomotive, no. 25260, with a train of empty mineral wagons emerges from the South Staffordshire line at Pleck Junction on the approach to Walsall, 6 September 1977. Note the power box, brought into use in the mid-1960s, and the Pleck Loop curving away to the left to provide direct access to Wolverhampton via the Grand Junction line (see top of page 51). (Michael Mensing.)

Access to the South Staffordshire line was provided at a number of junctions along the line. Ex-LMS class 4 2–6–0 no. 43040 joins the South Staffordshire line at Bescot Curve Junction (now obscured by the M6 motorway), *c.* 1960. This curve enabled trains from Bescot yard to have direct access to the line in a Dudley-bound direction. (Nigel Hazlewood.)

Above: ex-LMS 'Patriot' class 4–6–0 no. 45544 – as seen from Mesty Croft signal-box – climbs past Brunswick Park, Wednesbury, and the South Staffordshire Water Company's pumping station on its way to Dudley, *c.* 1960. *Below*: Mesty Croft signal-box on the climb to Wednesbury, *c.* 1960. This perfect example of the standard LNWR timber signal-box closed on 28 March 1966. (Both pictures: Nigel Hazlewood.)

An Ivatt 2–4–2T no. 41223, propelling 'The Dudley Dasher' auto-train from Dudley to Walsall, leaves Wednesbury Town station, towards the end of the 1950s. This passenger service lasted until the end of June 1964. (Collection of Roger Carpenter.)

This view of Wednesbury Town station shows the level-crossing at Potters Lane, the timber yard on the right, the basic layout of the station and – in the misty distance – the no. 2 signal-box and St John's Church. Everything, including the church, has now disappeared. (Nigel Hazlewood.)

Wednesbury no. 1 signal-box stood by the Potters Lane level-crossing, photographed here on 17 March 1993, two days before closure of the line, as class 37 locomotive no. 37026 and a 'rodless' 08 shunter pass through on a crew training trip. (Ned Williams.)

A class 45 locomotive crosses Potters Lane, Wednesbury, with a trip working, 1969. Note the footbridge by the crossing was still in place at this time. Lines to the Exchange Sidings are on the extreme right. (David Wilson.)

Ex-LNWR 0–8–0 no. 49173 shunts on the South Staffordshire line while an unidentified ex-GWR 'County' class locomotive crosses the scene with a northbound freight on the GWR main line, 10 August 1963. (Ralph Amos.)

Standing on the GWR embankment on the spot occupied by the 'County' in the above picture, the photographer has recorded a van train leaving the South Staffordshire line to take the Princes End line, c. 1960. The power station at Ocker Hill, and its cooling towers, dominates the landscape. The ground under water is now crossed by the Black Country Spine Road. Note the bogie steel-carrying wagons on the loop to the Exchange Sidings. (David Wilson.)

Ex-LMS 'Black Five' 4–6–0 no. 44807 climbs the steep bank away from Wednesbury, crosses the canal, and reaches Goldshill Crossing, *c.* 1960. (Eric Rogers.)

Goldshill Crossing box was another example of the perfectly proportioned LNWR standard design, but unlike the Mesty Croft box, it had a brick plinth. Its remote location gave good views of typical Black Country landscapes, eastwards to Wednesbury, westwards to Great Bridge, straight ahead into Ocker Hill Power Station, and backwards, over the wall, into Cashmore's Yard. (Nigel Hazlewood.)

Cashmore's Yard, between Goldshill Crossing and Eagle Lane crossing, became well known to railway enthusiasts when several batches of withdrawn locomotives were scrapped by the company. Here, ex-LMS 'Black Five' no. 45224 and BR class 2 no. 78055 await the torch, *c*. 1960. (G. Parkes.)

Eagle Lane Crossing, looking back towards Wednesbury, 9 March 1993 – ten days before closure of the line, as an unidentified class 47 locomotive crosses Eagle Lane with the return local trip working to Bescot. Cashmore's Yard has vanished from the landscape along with the coal-fired power station and cooling towers at Ocker Hill. The Spine Road now fills this view. (Ned Williams.)

Ex-GWR 0–6–2T no. 6646 passes through the South Staffordshire line station at Great Bridge North with a train of mineral wagons, while ex-LMS class 8F 2–8–0 no. 48762 stands in the loop waiting to act as 'banker', pushing heavy trains up the bank to Dudley *c.* 1960. Where Ratcliff's works stood, in the background, has now become a housing estate! (Nigel Hazlewood.)

Ex-GWR 2–6–2T no. 4167 on a Birmingham–Dudley train has just joined the South Staffordshire line at Horseley Fields Junction, 8 June 1963 – a year before the service was withdrawn. The signal-box protecting this junction can be seen on the embankment to the left of the picture. (Ralph Amos.)

At Dudley Port Low Level station, the South Staffordshire line passed under the Stour Valley main line – the latter with its Dudley Port High Level station, forming the background to this picture as a Western Region single-unit diesel car plus a driving trailer pass through Low Level non-stop with the 18.00 train from Dudley to Birmingham, 25 July 1959. (Michael Mensing.)

Ex-LMS 'Crab' class 2–6–0 no. 42799 on an excursion to Dudley Zoo, passes Palethorpes' Siding between Dudley Port and Sedgeley Junction, c. 1961. The spur from Dudley Port can be seen descending on the left. (David Wilson.)

Above: an ex-LNWR 0–8–0 stands at Sedgeley Junction with a train of Palethorpes' Sausages vans (a four-wheeler, three six-wheelers and a bogie vehicle), *c.* 1930. (Collection of John Dunn.) *Below*: Sedgeley Junction was in Tipton and employed its own spelling of Sedgley. It was destroyed by fire on 20 September 1964, shortly after being taken out of use. (Nigel Hazlewood.)

The South Staffordshire line was often used to bring excursionists to Dudley Zoo. Ex-LMS 'Jubilee' class 4–6–0 no. 45579, *Punjab*, climbs the last part of the bank into Dudley with a zoo excursion from Ambergate, 17 May 1964. (Paul Dorney.)

A two-car DMU waits to take the South Staffordshire line to Walsall with the 16.18 departure from Dudley, 26 August 1961. The service was withdrawn on 6 July 1964, the last passenger service provided from Dudley station. (Michael Mensing.)

A branch of the South Staffordshire line was the Princes End Loop from Wednesbury to Bloomfield Junction near Tipton Owen Street on the Stour Valley line, opened on 14 September 1863. Two short-lived passenger services were provided, and the line provided a useful detour when other lines were closed. Seen here on 30 October 1980, it has been singled, and class 25 locomotive no. 25209 is about to leave Ocker Hill for Wednesbury. (Robert Selvey.)

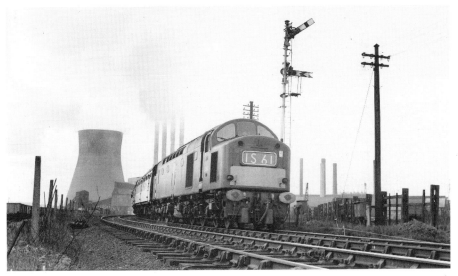

An unidentified class 40 locomotive passes the sidings at Ocker Hill Power Station with a diverted train using the Princes End Loop, c. 1960. (David Wilson.)

Another line that joined the South Staffordshire line was the ex-GWR line from Horseley Fields Junction (see page 63) to Swan Village on the GWR main line, opened on 1 September 1866. Ex-GWR 2–6–2T no. 5185 has just left the South Staffordshire line with the 17.08 Dudley–Birmingham train and is entering Great Bridge South station, 20 August 1957. (Collection of Roger Carpenter.)

From the other direction, ex-GWR 0–6–2T no. 5658 approaches Great Bridge South station from Birmingham, 17 June 1963. (Peter Shoesmith.)

An ex-GWR 0–6–2T leaves Swan Village for Great Bridge and Dudley against a backdrop of the wooden Swan Village gas holder, *c.* 1960. (David Wilson.)

Ex-GWR railcar no. W8 arrives at Swan Village from Dudley, June 1957. The new concrete footbridge is a sign that the station is about to be modernized. The new West Box, of 1952 vintage, can be seen in the background. (John Green.)

The Stourbridge Extension opened in stages from Stourbridge towards the GWR main line near Handsworth & Smethwick and seems to have become one of the few Black Country lines to maintain a high level of local commuter patronage. A class 25 locomotive is seen here taking the 'Extension' line from Stourbridge, with the North Box in the background on the far side of the West Midland line tracks, late 1960s. (John Dew.)

The first station on the 'Extension' was Lye, which, like Ely, claimed to have the shortest station nameboards in the country! Ex-GWR 'Grange' class 4–6–0 no. 6861, *Crynant Grange*, arrives at Lye with a stopping train to Worcester, early 1960s. (John Dew.)

The 'Extension' opened to Cradley on 1 April 1862, but as of 1 July 1899, the station was known as 'Cradley Heath & Cradley', recognizing that these were two distinct communities living on opposite banks of the Stour, and therefore in different counties. As the station had staggered platforms until recent times, the legend was that each community had its own platform. This picture was taken on 25 March 1962. (Ron Moss.)

Ex-GWR diesel railcar no. W22W parked in Cradley Heath goods yard, March 1962. The Earl of Dudley's Railway had a connection with the GWR at the far end of this yard. The site of the large goods shed seen here is now occupied by a bus station, built to encourage interchange between trains and buses, reflecting the commuter traffic found on the 'Extension'. (Ron Moss.)

An Intercity 125 HST unit passes through Cradley Heath station with a York–Plymouth train, which has been diverted via the 'Extension' as a result of Sunday engineering work on its usual route, 12 February 1984. (Peter Green.)

The 'Extension' reached Old Hill on 1 January 1866, and the station eventually became a junction for the Dudley and Halesowen lines. Ex-GWR 0-6-2T no. 6683 approaches Old Hill with a football supporters' train bound for The Hawthorns, 30 April 1960. The line to Dudley curves away to the right. (John Dew.)

On 1 April 1876, the 'Extension' was completed from Old Hill to Handsworth Junction, with stations at Rowley Regis, Langley Green, Rood End (closed 1885) and Smethwick Junction. Langley became a junction for the Oldbury branch, seen curving to the left in the foreground, as a DMU makes for Birmingham, 3 September 1966. (Peter Shoesmith.)

On 17 September 1956, Smethwick Junction was renamed Smethwick West, and it will be replaced by the new Galton Bridge Interchange station. Ex-GWR 2–6–2T no. 4105 passes Smethwick West with a freight train, 25 September 1960. (Michael Mensing.)

Returning to Langley Green, this picture clearly shows the now singled Oldbury Branch in the foreground. In the background, two class 31 locomotives prepare to shunt wagons into Rood End yard before taking them to Handsworth for scrapping. The men on the left are inspecting the remains of the frame from Langley Green Middle signal-box, demolished the previous day, 1 November 1993. (Paul Dorney.)

Class 31 locomotive no. 31198 with a train of Procur tankers makes its way along the Oldbury branch to its present terminus at Tat Bank, with the ICI works on the skyline, 11 June 1984. (Ned Williams.)

Returning to Old Hill station, this view from Beauty Bank reveals the Halesowen Branch platform and the sharp curve that took the line out of Old Hill and into Gorsty Hill Tunnel. In the foreground is one of the many rope-worked inclines used between Black Country pits and their canal-side wharves. (Author's collection.)

The line from Old Hill to Halesowen opened on 1 March 1878, and the GWR was joined at Halesowen by the Midland Railway when they opened their line from the south on 10 September 1883. In this view, the GWR is represented by a steam railcar, introduced on the line in 1905, and the Midland by a Johnson 0–4–4T and train on the centre road. Both pictures were taken in about 1910. (Author's collection.)

The Halesowen Branch spawned its own branch – to Halesowen Canal Basin, opened on 2 April 1902. The line closed on 1 October 1969, and ex-GWR 0–6–PT no. 4698 is seen at the basin a year earlier – the twilight of steam! (John Dew.)

The Halesowen line lost its passenger services at the end of 1927, but workmen's trains continued to use the line to reach the Austin Works at Longbridge. It was also popular on enthusiasts' specials. An 'SLS Special' is seen at Halesowen, behind ex-LMS 2F 0–6–0 no. 58271, 30 May 1959. (John Dew.)

The line from Old Hill to Dudley, known as the 'Bumble Hole Line', or 'Windmill End Branch', opened on 1 March 1878. Its rather quaint train service, partly steam-worked, lasted until 13 June 1964 and attracted photographers who liked an offbeat challenge. Ex-GWR 0–6–0PT no. 6403 waits at Old Hill station with the 12.45 Saturdays Only train, 1962. (David Wilson.)

Ex-GWR 0–6–0PT no. 7443, leaves Old Hill High Street Halt for Old Hill, 29 April 1963. The halts on the line acquired these simple shelters in the mid-1950s, replacing slightly more substantial structures. (David Wilson.)

Ex-GWR diesel railcar no. W8W pauses at Windmill End Halt, May 1956. Windmill End had once boasted bigger buildings than the other halts and had even been a station with stationmaster and staff. The replacement shelter was therefore a little more grand than those at the other halts. (Collection of Roger Carpenter.)

A BR diesel single-car unit approaches Baptist End Halt as a train from Old Hill, 31 August 1962. Behind the train is Windmill End Junction and the goods-only branch to Withymoor Basin (Netherton Goods). (Peter Shoesmith.)

Ex-GWR 0–6–0PT no. 9646 stands at Withymoor Basin (Netherton Goods), by the Northfield Road crossing, 1964. The line opened on 10 March 1879 and closed on 5 July 1965. (Ned Williams.)

A BR diesel single-car unit approaches Blowers Green Junction, as seen from the New Road overbridge, 29 April 1963. The long shadow is a reminder that photographers could only record this train service first thing in the morning, in the early evening, or as the one lunch-time train on Saturdays. (David Wilson.)

The last train from Old Hill, seen at Dudley station after its historic trip on 13 June 1964. Ex-GWR 0-6-0PT no. 7418 from Wolverhampton was in charge of the normal one-coach train – on this occasion, packed to capacity! (Graham Sidwell.)

Stourbridge Junction is another of those stations that has been moved around and much altered over the years, since the OWWR first arrived in 1852. Even the Stourbridge Town Branch of 1879 first made its way into a junction to the north of the present station, which was opened on this site in October 1901. The branch was re-aligned, and in this form has served the town ever since. An ex-GWR 0–6–0PT leaves the junction, 2 November 1963. (John Dew.)

The history of the branch is further complicated by starting life as a double-track line, changed in 1935 to two parallel single lines – one for goods trains proceeding to the yard, the other for passenger trains halting at Stourbridge Town station. Today, it is a conventional single-track branch, but Stourbridge Town station has moved slightly towards the junction! Ex-GWR 0–6–0PT no. 7429 traverses the branch with a circus train, 16 October 1955. (John Dew.)

Stourbridge has a great deal of interesting railway history – the branch from the junction to the town station (opened on 1 October 1879, and still open today), the canal basin, goods yard, gas works, etc. at 'Lower Stourbridge' and the engine shed virtually in Amblecote. Ex-GWR 0–4–2T no. 1414 stands at Stourbridge, about to propel its one-coach auto-train back to the junction, 9 September 1957. (John Dew.)

Ex-GWR 0–4–2T no. 1414 seen from the town end of Stourbridge station in the 1950s. The line on the left continued down a steep bank to the goods yard and canal basin, which had originally (before 1879/80) been reached by an incline from the OWWR/West Midland line by Stourbridge Shed. (John Dew.)

An ex-GWR 0–6–0PT climbs the 1 in 27 band from the goods yard to Stourbridge Town station, 8 April 1961. The line closed on 20 September 1965, the last train having run at the end of April. (John Dew.)

A general view of facilities at Stourbridge Town Goods station, including the canal transhipment shed and the gas works on the right. In the background is the railway company's building, which faced Amblecote Road. A line crossed this road, including its one-time tram tracks, and made its way alongside the Stour to Bradley's Ironworks. (John Dew.)

Kingswinford Junction on the West Midland line (see top of page 35) was the beginning of an interesting branch, which first opened as an OWWR line from the junction to Bromley Basin on 14 November 1858. Over the next few years, this was extended northwards, and in the twentieth century it became a through line to Oxley Junction on the Wolverhampton–Shrewsbury line. This view of the junction shows a double-headed train waiting to come off the branch as 0–6–0PT no. 9608 passes on the main line, 1966. (Paul Dorney.)

The southern portion of this line, from Kingswinford Junction up to the Oak Farm/Shut End area north of Pensnett, was first known as the 'Kingswinford Branch' – hence the name of the junction. It served an area well populated with pits, brickyards and ironworks, and over the years was linked to numerous sidings and industrial lines. 0–6–0PT no. 3607 makes its way through this landscape between Brockmoor and Bromley, 29 June 1966. (Paul Dorney.)

Bromley Basin, with the canal transhipment shed on the left and Bromley Basin signal-box in the distance, looking northwards. This photograph was taken in about 1962; the box closed on 17 December 1967. (Paul Dorney.)

A rare visit by an enthusiast special seemed to mark the final demise of the branch. The Branch Line Society special crawls through Bromley Halt, with class 47s, no. 47838 leading and no. 47489 propelling, 23 February 1991. (Ned Williams.)

Ex-GWR 0–6–0PT no. 9614 pauses between shunting duties at Pensnett, by the signal-box, 18 June 1966. The picture reveals the extent to which the line dipped under the main Dudley–Kingswinford road at this point. (Paul Birchill.)

Looking back towards Bromley from the bridge seen above, we see ex-GWR 0–6–0PT no. 3658 arriving at Pensnett with the Saturday morning trip working from the junction to Baggeridge Junction, just north of Pensnett, 18 May 1963. Note the grass-grown platforms (the last passenger train called in 1932!), the uprights that once held the name-board and the signal-box, the top of which is now preserved at Bridgnorth. (David Wilson.)

The Coal Concentration Depot opened at Pensnett in 1964 (see page 104), but declined in use during the 1980s miners' strike. Here, Lunt, Comley & Pitt's 0–4–0 diesel shunter, *Peter*, shunts a few wagons arriving at Pensnett in the wake of the dispute, 9 July 1985. (Robert Selvey.)

Pensnett, 11 March 1988. The Coal Concentration Depot in the background seems abandoned, but some low-sided wagons of pig iron have arrived. Class 45 locomotive no. 45058 shunts some wagons of Perrier Water into the siding alongside a hastily constructed unloading bay – the last chapter in the ever-changing goods traffic handled by the branch, inaugurated on 5 June 1986. (Ned Williams.)

Ex-GWR 'Grange' class 4–6–0 no. 6876, *Kingsland Grange*, rounds the curve between Baggeridge Junction and Gornal Halt on 8 February 1964 with one of the Crewe–Worcester through trains that made good use of the line until its closure in 1965. (David Wilson.)

Ex-GWR 'Modified Hall' class 4–6–0 no. 6972, *Beningbrough Hall*, at Baggeridge Junction, 1962. Note the signal-box partly obscured by the train, and the line curving away to the right. The latter provided access to the line to Baggeridge Colliery, and, by reversing at Askew Bridge, to the Pensnett Railway – the Earl of Dudley's system. (David Wilson.)

At Baggeridge Junction, the line singled and became quite rural in character. This stretch through to Oxley was the final product of various attempts to link Wolverhampton with Bridgnorth, via Wombourn. The Wombourn–Bridgnorth part of the plan never materialized, but this section did, opening as recently as 1925. Here, ex-GWR 'Hall' class 4–6–0 no. 6946, *Heatherden Hall*, pauses at Wombourn, 8 February 1964. (David Wilson.)

Ganger Dan Brew at Wombourn with his motorized platelayers' inspection trolley, ?late 1930s. To the left of the picture stood the Wombourn signal-box, with its name-board confirming that the GWR wished to spell Wombourn without a final 'e'. Wombourn was the only passing place between Baggeridge Junction and Oxley. (Peter Brew.)

Tettenhall station, as the first passenger train inaugurates the short-lived service, 11 May 1925. GWR steam railcars were used, and the timetable was eventually organized so that the service could be provided by one railcar. Tettenhall's second platform was never used, and the redundant footbridge was soon removed. (P. Eisenhoffer.)

BR class 25 no. D6157 stands at Tettenhall on track-lifting duties, 31 December 1967. The line from Oxley to Baggeridge Junction was closed from 1 March 1965. The trackbed has become a public footpath, and the main station building has become a wardens' centre. (David Smith.)

Before the Wombourn line joined the Wolverhampton–Shrewsbury, it doubled and split at Oxley Branch Junction. One double track then curved towards the west and joined the main line at Oxley North Junction, the other curved east and joined the main line at Oxley Middle Junction. A train can be seen here taking the curve towards Oxley North, 2 July 1964. (David Wilson.)

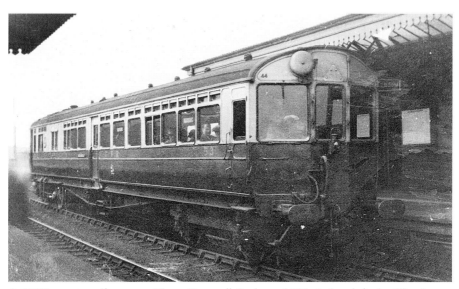

A GWR steam railcar, no. 53, at Dunstall Park, *c.* 1930. It has left the Wombourn Branch at Oxley Middle Junction and is in the process of making its way to Wolverhampton Low Level station. Nearly all trains on the branch ran between Low Level and Stourbridge Junction. (Fred Braybrook.)

Two other 'byways' in the Wolverhampton area deserve a mention. Once the GWR had reached the Shrewsbury line via its line from Wolverhampton Low Level station and Cannock Road Junction, the former S&BR line to Victoria Basin became a backwater. Herbert Street Goods Depot was built on land close to the canal basin. Even when the canal basin was no longer served by rail traffic and Herbert Street was replaced by larger facilities in 1931, the branch was still called the Victoria Basin Branch, and the small signal-box seen here in 1962 was called Victoria Basin signal-box. The picture looks back towards Stafford Road Junction. On the right can be seen the ex-LNWR main line north of Wolverhampton High Level station. (Eric Hamilton.)

In 1966, Wolverhampton North Junction was created to allow trains from Wolverhampton High Level station to gain access to the former Victoria Basin Branch and to make for Shrewsbury. By the time Wolverhampton Low Level station had been demoted to a parcels depot in 1970, the line from there to Cannock Road Junction had been removed. Coal trains from the north wishing to reach the Shrewsbury line had to reverse at Cannock Road. All this eventually led to rationalization and a new piece of railway line – the 'Oxley Chord' – seen here as no. D200 operates a special over the new line (opened in August 1983), 18 February 1985. (Brian Robbins.)

The Wolverhampton–Walsall line of the Midland Railway opened on 1 November 1872, providing the Midland Railway with intermediate stations at Heath Town, Wednesfield, Willenhall, Short Heath, Bentley and North Walsall. It lost its passenger service on 5 January 1931 and attracted few photographers. A picture of a train on the line is very rare, but on 10 July 1958, ex-LMS 2P 4–4–0 was caught at Wednesfield with the District Engineer's inspection train. The last train to Wednesfield ran in March 1981. (Tim Shuttleworth.)

Access to the stations at Wednesfield and Willenhall was from road overbridges, which also provided photographic vantage points for views such as this one of Wednesfield, c. 1960. The Ductile Steel Company's factory in the background was served by the line, and the company had their own diesel shunter. (David Wilson.)

Willenhall's Midland Railway station, as seen *c*. 1960. It was known as 'Willenhall Market Place' or 'Willenhall Stafford Street', to distinguish it from the LNWR station. This was the only line in the Black Country where the standard MR signal-boxes could be found. (Collection of Roger Carpenter.)

Short Heath station, looking towards Walsall, *c*. 1960. It was located at the point where the line crossed Clark's Lane – now the site of a fire station. Behind the main station building, a siding ran to the local gas works. The line was 'severed' in 1964 by the M6, and both sections then withered away! (David Wilson.)

Section Five

ON THE SHED

Locomotive sheds have a particular fascination for enthusiasts, and the Black Country provided quite a variety of sheds which one could dream of visiting. Some sheds housed locomotives on passenger duties, some on goods duties, and some housed both. However, the distinction that was probably more important to enthusiasts at the time was their company of origin. Thus GWR or BR Western Region enthusiasts would have been drawn to Wolverhampton's Stafford Road and Oxley sheds, or the isolated shed at Stourbridge. LMS or BR London Midland Region enthusiasts would have been drawn to Bescot and Ryecroft, in the Walsall area, or Bushbury, at Wolverhampton.

All the sheds mentioned above are illustrated in this section, and only one survives in any form – Bescot Diesel Depot, dating from the mid-1960s, but built almost on the site of the steam shed. However, the Black Country has, in the past played host to other locomotive sheds, which unfortunately are not illustrated here.

The Shrewsbury & Birmingham Railway opened a shed at Stafford Road when it reached Wolverhampton in 1849. In the same way, the other companies built small sheds at the limits of the lines they worked. Thus the OWWR built a shed at Low Level station, the Stour Valley Railway (LNWR) built a shed close to Queen Street (High Level) station, both in Wolverhampton. Other small sheds existed: for example, the OWWR had used locomotive sheds at Dudley and Stourbridge during the nineteenth century. The LNWR provided itself with a very tiny shed at Tipton – squeezed between the main line and the canal. The Midland Railway, when it arrived, provided itself with a shed in what became known as 'Midland Road'.

When the first generation of sheds became redundant and were replaced by the second generation of 'bigger and better' sheds, the former were sometimes put to other uses. For example, the shed north of Wolverhampton High Level station became a carriage shed, the shed at Dudley was literally moved to one side and became a goods shed.

In more recent times sheds had to adapt, or close, as diesel propulsion replaced steam and the network was rationalized. The demise of the sheds has had an effect on the way in which local towns could relate to the railway as a major employer and think of themselves, in part, as 'railway towns'. This is considered further in Section Seven.

Sheds were smoky, and the work that surrounded them was hard and dirty. Visitors were not always welcome. For these reasons, shed photographs have not been as easy to take as station scenes or line-side pictures. Therefore, we have to be particularly grateful to photographers who responded to this challenge and recorded the life and times of local sheds.

Black Country contrasts: LNWR 2–4–2T no. 2126, cleaners and crew pose proudly at Ryecroft Shed, Walsall, just after the First World War. The shed itself looks smart, the engine is polished, and the interest is very apparent. (Collection of Jack Haddock.)

By way of a contrast, the ex-GWR shed at Wolverhampton Stafford Road looks deserted and dilapidated in the late 1950s. This part of the shed was created by roofing over this area in the 1860s – indicating the way that Stafford Road mushroomed, rather than being built as a single, complete entity. However, it was the home of prestigious locomotives, including the GWR 'Kings'. In this scene, 'Castle' class no. 7026, *Sudeley Castle*, and 'Hall' class no. 6969, *Wraysbury Hall*, are in residence. (Fred Braybrook.)

Wolverhampton's Oxley Shed was opened in July 1907 on the north-western fringe of the town. It provided accommodation for GWR freight locomotives on tracks radiating from two turntables. This picture, looking towards one of the turntables, shows ex-GWR class 47xx 2–8–0 no. 4701 at rest, 1 March 1959. The locomotive carries an 81A shed plate, suggesting that its normal home was Old Oak Common. (Ron Moss.)

An ex-Ministry of Supply, War Department, 2–8–0 locomotive no. 90693 stands outside the western end of Oxley Shed on the through road, 18 October 1959. The large red brick building featured three gables, and the long side elevation overlooked the racecourse. Until March 1976, when the shed closed, race-goers could train their binoculars on locomotive movements at the shed between races. (L. Hanson.)

The GWR's passenger locomotive shed in Wolverhampton was Stafford Road, and it had a much more complex history and track layout than the shed at Oxley. At its height, Stafford Road consisted of a straight road shed and a turntable shed with tracks served by three turntables. At the turn of the century, the rather cramped conditions at Stafford Road were relieved by the provision of the Lower Yard, and the coaling, watering and turning of locomotives was clearly visible from Foxes Lane, thus making this a much-photographed location. Scenes photographed inside the shed are rarer, but ex-GWR 0–6–0PTs no. 3683 and no. 6418 are seen here, 10 June 1961. The shed closed in September 1963. (Norman Glover.)

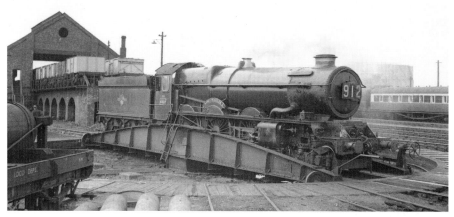

The coaling and turning of engines at Stafford Road Shed, Lower Yard, mentioned above, can be seen here as ex-GWR 'King' class 4–6–0 no. 6010, *King Charles I*, stands on the turntable, with the coaler in the left background, 18 October 1959. On the right, looking across the tracks of the Wolverhampton–Shrewsbury main line, are the Cannock Road Carriage Sidings. Beyond is a gas holder, the only feature of this scene to have survived until the 1990s. (L. Hanson.)

Bushbury Shed was the LMS shed in Wolverhampton, once again situated on the northern side of the town, not very far from the rival GWR sheds. It was provided by the LNWR in the 1880s, replacing an earlier, small timber shed which in turn had replaced a shed just north of High Level station, but it never grew to the size of the GWR sheds or received the same attention from photographers. It closed in 1965. This view is looking towards the shed, with Bushbury Lane crossing the picture behind it, 1920s. (Collection of Eric Hamilton.)

Ex-LMS 'Ivatt' class 2 2–6–0 no. 46430 stands at Bushbury, 1960s. In the background is the coaling tower, providing some automation to this activity, which seemed very modern compared with the coaling facilities at the rival sheds. (Simon Dewey.)

Ex-GWR class 63xx 2–6–0 no. 6349, outside Stourbridge Shed, 18 October 1959. The first shed, a four-road straight shed, opened in 1870, but the larger, brick-built shed seen here was not completed and opened until 1926 – and then only lasted forty years! The two chimneys apparently rising from no. 6349's cab are attached to the shed's two stationary boilers. (L. Hanson.)

After closure, a deserted Stourbridge Shed plays host to ex-GWR 'Collett' class 2251 0–6–0 no. 3205 on its way to Kidderminster, where it was about to become the first steam locomotive to work on the preserved Severn Valley Railway, 24 March 1967. (Joe Challingsworth.)

The LNWR built a small shed at Ryecroft on the eastern approach to Walsall, exploiting their standard design with north-light roof, placing the turntable, as can be seen here, at the rear of the shed. Although photographed in the 1950s, the LNWR atmosphere of this scene is enhanced by 2–4–2T no. 46757. These pre-grouping veterans survived into the BR period on local services from Walsall to Dudley and Wolverhampton. (Eric Rogers.)

The Midland Railway also provided itself with a small engine shed in Walsall, and it is just visible in this view of the western approach to Walsall station, early 1960s. The shed had closed in about 1925. Ex-LMS Stanier 2–6–0 no. 42974 brings a train past the Midland Shed and the carriage sidings with one of the last regular steam passenger workings through Walsall: a Birmingham (Aston)–Brownhills train. (Jack Haddock.)

Bescot Shed was opened by the LNWR in 1892, as the surrounding land was consumed by an expanding marshalling yard. Both shed and yard remained a focal point in the local railway network until the 1990s, long after other sheds and yards had disappeared into history. This picture looks across the locomotive sidings towards Bescot station and shows an interesting variety of 0–8–0, 0–6–0, and 0–6–2T locomotives of distinctive LNWR outline, 26 May 1931. (L. Hanson.)

Another picture taken from the same spot about thirty years later shows locomotives with a greater LMS and Midland style, but the ubiquitous 'Duck Eight' outline of an ex-LNWR 0–8–0 can be seen behind no. 58181's chimney! The most obvious addition to the scene is the coaling equipment and ash plant, added in the mid-1930s. (Eric Rogers.)

RAILWAYS IN THE

SERVICE OF INDUSTRY

The first pages in this section illustrate some of the goods traffic and goods facilities that the railway companies provided in the Black Country – most of which were related to the needs of the local industry. We then move on to look at the railway systems that industries provided internally for their own use.

It is not possible to survey the railways of the Black Country without making some attempt to include the railways that formed internal systems within local industrial complexes. As pointed out in the Introduction, a private industrial railway system, the Earl of Dudley's Railway, was the first in the region and grew to be one of the lengthiest of such railways in the country. It included the internal railway system of the Round Oak Steel Works, but its tentacles stretched from Cradley Heath Goods Yard in the south to Baggeridge Colliery in the north, from Ashwood Basin in the west to Wellington Road, Dudley, in the east. Even today, two or three ex-Round Oak shunters work at the private sidings of the Round Oak Steel Terminal, a few yards from the 'new world' of Merry Hill and The Waterfront!

During the nineteenth century, many short 'tramroads', narrow gauge railways, standard gauge railways and sidings were built to serve the ever-changing transport needs of local industry. Some of these were very short indeed and were traversed by hand-pushed tubs between pitheads and canal wharves. Others were horse-worked or used rope haulage. Some grew into complex systems serving collieries, canal wharves and furnaces and the links to the nearest main line railway, and acquired their own locomotives and rolling stock. The best-known systems were the ones that served the large ironworks that grew into twentieth-century steelworks at Bilston and Wednesbury. (Round Oak has already been mentioned.) These survived into more recent times and were therefore comparatively well photographed. We have much less visual information on the lines at Corngreaves, Cradley Heath or the Pelsall Ironworks, or the Hatherton Furnaces. (For a dip into this esoteric world of local industrial lines, the reader should seek out the Industrial Railway Society's *Industrial Locomotives of the West Midlands*.)

Quarries, factories, and gas works, even sewage works, were also potential users of railway systems. For example, the Courtaulds Factory in Wolverhampton, laid out as late as the mid-1920s, included a railway system with its own steam locomotives and a connection to the outside world of the GWR's system. Building contractors also used railways to build such things as the Wolverhampton–Birmingham New Road, or large inter-war housing estates. The Pensnett Industrial Estate, developed in the 1950s, included sidings laid to factory sites and a connection to the main line railway. Traffic included components for the motor industry.

Today, we think of road haulage as being the important industrial beast of burden, and developers are more likely to think of motorway access than to contemplate building a railway siding or an internal railway system. Not only has the private industrial railway virtually disappeared from the Black Country, the public railway has also declined locally in terms of serving local industry. Steel termini still exist at Wolverhampton and Brierley Hill, but coal and oil depots have disappeared; Dudley Freightliner Depot closed after a working life of less than twenty years.

An aerial view of Shut End, near Pensnett, 1959. Running from left to right across the top of the scene is the Kingswinford Junction–Oxley Junction line, via Wombourn. On the far side of the line is the Coal Concentration Depot opened in 1964 and the wartime buildings that were used in the early days of the Pensnett Trading Estate. In the nineteenth century, this area had been part of the Shut End Iron Works, and the bridge visible top right had once carried the Earl of Dudley's line over the GWR line. In the foreground is the Dreadnought Works, a tile factory served by two sidings just visible by the course of the earl's line. In this one small area, the railways are seen in juxtaposition to the sometime coal, iron and brick and tile industries. (Author's collection.)

A train of iron ore from Northamptonshire is seen on the way to Stewarts & Lloyds Steelworks, Bilston, passing through West Bromwich, 18 April 1963. The locomotive in charge is ex-GWR 'Grange' class 4–6–0 no. 6830, *Buckenhill Grange*. (Ralph Amos.)

A train of coal from Baggeridge Colliery sets out for its journey to Stourport Power Station – seen here passing through Pensnett Halt, 2 July 1966. The locomotive in charge is ex-GWR 0–6–0PT no. 8718, the last surviving class 57xx locomotive with the original type of cab. (Paul Burchill.)

Railway marshalling yards play a vital part in moving goods traffic from local trains into long-distance trains. The GWR yards at Oxley and Stourbridge Junction have gone, but the yards at Bescot still survive, although many local trip workings into the Black Country now seem to come from further afield. This was the signalman's view of Bescot Down Yard from Bescot no. 5 box, early 1960s. (Nigel Hazlewood.)

In the mid-1960s, Bescot Yard was completely laid out afresh as a hump-marshalling yard controlled from modern power boxes. This was the view from the Down control tower during 1964, with Bescot station and motive power depot in the distance. (Nigel Hazlewood.)

Steel termini in the Black Country: 1. The Wednesbury Steel Terminal was established on what had once been the GWR main line just north of Wednesbury, and access from the South Staffordshire line was via the Exchange Sidings once used for exchange of wagons between the GWR and LMS systems. Class 45 diesel locomotive no. 45012 stands at the terminal, having arrived on the trip working from Bescot, 14 May 1984. This view has changed dramatically as the Black Country Spine Road has made its way from Great Bridge towards Moxley. (Ned Williams.)

2. During the 1980s, the Wolverhampton Steel Terminal was often full, and spare capacity was made available by using the sidings into what had been the canal basin at Monmore Green. The track in the foreground also provided access to sidings used at the time by the British Oxygen Company. Class 08 diesel shunter no. 08466 is slowly shunting at Monmore Green, 6 June 1984. (Ned Williams.)

3. Space continued to be a problem at Wolverhampton Steel Terminal into the 1990s, and for a short time the former Midland Railway Goods Depot at Wednesfield Road was used to transfer steel to road transport. Here, class 37 diesel locomotive no. 37038 is seen at Wednesfield Road with a trip working from Washwood Heath, March 1990. Since then, all traffic to Wednesfield Road has ceased, and the Goods Depot awaits redevelopment as part of the Black Country Development Corporation's 'Heritage Junction' site. (Paul Dorney.)

Scrap once played a part in feeding local furnaces, and one of the last scrap metal rail-users was Norton Barrow (Metals) Ltd of Loxdale Street, Bilston. Here, class 08 diesel shunter no. 08603 has arrived at Norton's with a single wagon having just traversed the single line from Wednesbury along what had once been the GWR main line. This track was last used on 30 August 1992, when a special train from Bescot Open Day made it to within a few hundred yards of this point! (Ned Williams.)

The iron-producing industry of the Black Country had boomed in the middle of the nineteenth century and declined by the 1880s. Some ironworks were redeveloped as steelworks, and such sites have a complex history, including a bewildering number of changes to such things as canal basins, narrow gauge tramroads, sidings and access to standard gauge main line railways. These two views of the Bilston Steelworks site show (above) the scene at Stewarts & Lloyds inherited as they took control of Alfred Hickman Ltd in the 1920s, and (below) the new plant that developed and after the Second World War, including 'Elizabeth', the single blast furnace. (Author's collection.)

British Steel continued to operate the Bilston Steelworks until 1978/79 and continued to make great use of the internal railways system until that time. Like all such systems, it featured tight curves and tracks that curved round or burrowed beneath every other kind of structure. Diesel locomotives were introduced from 1952 onwards, and no. 9, seen here in 1976 in typical steelworks setting, dated from 1960 (Yorkshire Engine Co. no. 2796). It was one of the last survivors of the fleet, being cut up on the abandoned site in 1983. (Nick Hedges.)

Yorkshire Engine Co. diesel shunter no. 2, *Philip* (no. 2507 of 1953), on a train of slag-carrying wagons at Bilston Steelworks, June 1971. (Nostalgia, Stechford.)

Typical of the locomotives used at Bilston was 0–4–0ST *Patricia* (Andrew Barclay no. 1842 of 1924, scrapped 1965). (Norman Glover.)

Bilston Steelworks had its own railway shed and workshops, and three Yorkshire Engine 0–4–0 diesel shunters are seen here in the maintenance department as the plant began to contract and close down, 1 July 1978. (Gordon Nutt.)

Andrew Barclay 0–4–0STs were popular at all three major Black Country steelworks, and Patent Shaft Steelworks no. 8 (no. 1064 of 1906) was typical of the breed but managed to look even more 'chunky' with dumb buffers. (Collection of the IRS.)

Lady Patricia (Andrew Barclay no. 1880 of 1925) was another of these engines, in this case working at the Round Oak Steel Works, mid-1930s. Note the fully lined green livery. *Lady Patricia* is shown here at The Wallows and stands cab-to-cab with one of the larger 0–6–0 saddle tanks built by Andrew Barclay for work on the Barrow Hill Incline and the line to Baggeridge. (Collection of Roger Carpenter.)

Baggeridge Colliery started production in 1912 and was linked by the Earl of Dudley's railway system to the works at Round Oak and to the GWR's lines at Baggeridge Junction. The sidings beneath the screens, seen here in the 1920s, are full of the Earl of Dudley's coal wagons, some of which went to Round Oak, others of which went to land sale wharves served by the railway. (Collection of Jim Evans.)

The line from Baggeridge Colliery was worked by the parent system until 1952. After that date, National Coal Board locomotives brought the coal down to Askew Bridge to hand over to either BR (via Baggeridge Junction) or the Round Oak Steelworks engine, as seen here on 26 September 1966, the last day coal was conveyed from there to Round Oak. Round Oak diesel shunter no. 10 (no. YE2883 of 1963) exchanges wagons with NCB 0–6–0ST no. 9 (Hunslet no. 3777 of 1952). (Collection of Viv Morgan.)

Gas works in Wolverhampton, Walsall and Swan Village had railway sidings extensive enough to justify having their own shunting locomotives. Diesels arrived at Swan Village in 1952, and no. 1 can be seen on the left – a new Andrew Barclay, works no. 386. In the background are no. 21 (Hudswell Clarke no. 1734 of 1943) and no. 20 (Peckett no. 2032 of 1942). (Phyl Lycett.)

Peckett no. 1897 (of 1936) is shown shunting at Walsall Gas Works, just west of Walsall station, 29 March 1967. (Ralph Amos.)

Section Seven

THE WORKERS

Most railway photographs show the system at work, but do not necessarily show the men and women who worked on the railway actually undertaking their tasks. Thus many pictures have no human interest at all – it is the machinery, infrastructure and system that is illustrated and is often the focus on our interest. Perhaps someone on the footplate of a passing engine is seen waving or smiling at the photographer, or the signalman is glimpsed at the windows of his box. Perhaps the distant outline of a porter is visible in a station scene.

The photographs in this section are intended to bring us a little closer to the men and women on the railway and to allow us to see them at work. If stations and locomotives are part of local history, then surely the same goes for those local people who manned them, and it is as important to identify a railwayman in a photograph as it is to record the name and number of a locomotive.

Looking through this small selection of pictures, there are several observations that can be made. First of all, it should be apparent that working on the railway encompassed an enormous variety of tasks, all with different traditions and skills. Second, it is visually apparent that each trade and occupation on the railway presented itself in a different manner, even in the way they dressed. The railway workforce was very hierarchical in its organization and rather rigidly divided. This has been reflected in trade union organization. The aristocratic 'craftsmen' of the railway were the footplatemen (eventually represented by what has become ASLEF). As in all such professions, progress was long and hard-going – serving for years as a cleaner, then for years as a fireman, and eventually becoming a driver. For some, working on the railway has been accompanied by the loftiest sense of vocation; for others it has meant long hours, dirty work and low pay.

The non footplate staff have now become associated with the NUR, but the membership of the NUR included people from many walks of railway life, and like all general unions, it has contained many factions. I have spoken to guards who felt they were misunderstood by signalmen, and vice versa! And I have spoken to booking clerks (represented by the TSSA) who felt they were misunderstood by the uniformed staff, and vice versa!

In the Black Country, several towns had working populations of which railway-workers were a significant proportion. This was true in Walsall, Stourbridge and particularly Wolverhampton. In Wolverhampton, there was added interest in this, in as much as the town was served by both the LMS and the GWR: it was not just a matter of being part of a railway family and railway community – it was a matter of to which particular company did you owe your loyalty?

To some extent, the railways have existed in their own semi-closed world, only glimpsed by outsiders who are passengers or nosey enthusiasts. Railwaymen even mixed exclusively with fellow railwaymen once they had left their work, and communities developed where railwaymen lived. Steelworkers and colliers had the same experience, but increased social mobility since the Second World War and the collapse of the world of work as we once knew it have changed all that.

This wonderful study of men and machine was taken, not on the main line railway system, but on the internal railway system of the Patent Shaft Steelworks at Wednesbury. The locomotive was called *Monway*, one of the constituent works of the Patent Shaft complex, and was built by Hawthorn Leslie in 1889 (works no. 2170). It spent its entire life at Patent Shaft until scrapped in 1951. Once again, dress codes and headgear seem important, but notice that the footplate crew wear collars and ties like their counterparts on the main line. (Collection of Black Country Society.)

Photographs taken by railwaymen of themselves working on the railway are fairly rare. An exceptional railwayman was Paddy Powderly, second from the right in this picture. He was a fitter at Stafford Road, Wolverhampton, and on several occasions in the 1940s he took his camera to work and recorded the scene. In this case, he handed the camera to a colleague, and the lads posed in front of 0–6–0PT no. 3760. The picture were taken just after the Second World War, but the locomotive is still carrying the black-out shield used to prevent light leaking from the footplate via the cab door.

Paddy Powderly's photographs were usually posed snaps of his fellow railwaymen, but a number of the pictures show quite a sense of location. In this case, his colleagues, including Jimmy Donnellan in the cap, have posed at the top of the steps that climbed to the entrance of the Railwaymen's Institute on Stafford Road. The building played host to a variety of users, including 'Improvement Classes' for the footplate staff, and, at one stage, the wages office. The steps far outlived the building and became a much-loved local landmark, only finally obliterated when Stafford Road recently became a dual carriageway.

To the left of the Railwaymen's Institute was the entrance to Stafford Road Works, and one morning, Paddy Powderly posed his mates in front of the entrance as other railway employees arrived for work on their bicycles. The no. 2 watertank was a prominent feature of the skyline at this location. (All three pictures from the collection of Mrs Joan Powderly.)

In 1960, the 'Birmingham Pullman' was introduced as a 7.00 a.m. departure from Wolverhampton to Paddington. Diesel Locomotive Training Instructor Ken Southern (left) poses at Cannock Road Coach Sidings with the driver who has just brought the new blue train up to Wolverhampton from Swindon in order to launch the new service. (Eric Hamilton.)

One of the commonest types of pictures depicting railwaymen are the 'Improvement Class' photographs. These classes were held in enginemen's own time but were essential training for any employee who wished to progress through the grades from cleaner to fireman to driver. Further progress was then through 'the links', from local shunting work to the driving of prestigious main line passenger expresses. The 1927 class at Stourbridge Shed is seen here in front of 'Duke' class 4–4–0 no. 3255. (Gron Evans.)

The 'Improvement Class' of 1935 at Stourbridge Shed pose in front of 'Hall' class 4–6–0 locomotive no. 4999, *Gospal Hall*. Note the model valve gear that has been added to the visual aids on display. The line-up seems to include everyone from schoolboys in caps (on the footplate) to distinguished senior railwaymen. One man sports a bow tie, while the engine crew seem dressed for 'real' work! (Collection of Dave Hadley.)

Presentations to railwaymen were photographed, but seldom in such a way as to reveal much railway location! On 12 July 1961, the winners in the annual railwaymen's motor parade were photographed at Wednesfield Road Goods Depot in Wolverhampton. Left to right: Rail Motor Driver Law (3rd prize), District Motor Engineer R.A. Tyrewhitt and Rail Motor Driver Albert Wright (1st prize) with his Austin delivery lorry (280 HRO), District Manager V.G. Petlow, Foreman A.G. Saunders and Rail Motor Driver H. Platt (2nd prize). (Collection of Roger Wright.)

Railway trade union activity has been little recorded in text or in pictures at a local level. Many railwaymen took any active part in union affairs, and this could lead into other areas of the Labour Movement, ranging from work in Co-operative Societies to party politics in local government. Here, we see Councillor E.J. Stokes (also Chairman of the NUR in Dudley) presenting a certificate to Alderman Charlie Williams to mark thirty-five years' service as Secretary of the Dudley Branch of the NUR, June 1948. Signalman Charlie Williams was an active trade unionist, twice mayor of Dudley, and a leading member of Dudley Co-operative Society. (Collection of Anne Thomas.)

Stationmaster H.W. Payton in GWR uniform at Halesowen, *c.* 1910. He won prizes for the station in GWR station garden competitions and ran his station with the discipline associated with the late Victorian railway system – staff were summoned by a whistle. Mr Payton was active in promoting Halesowen and its station and played an active part in local government. (Collection of Miss Payton.)

Station staff at Dudley Port on the Up platform, photographed by Signalman Cyril Hand towards the end of the 1950s. Left to right: Junior Porter Harry Bishop, Parcel Porter Hinsley, Inspector Jack Morris and an unidentified shunter. A station like Dudley Port could once have employed as many as forty people. (Cyril Hand.)

Railway signalmen, or 'bobbies', were rarely photographed at work as they were rather remote from public sight. Rules required that they gave 100 per cent attention to their work, so even signalmen who took their cameras to work rarely admitted taking any photographs. Signalman Cyril Hand did pause to take a picture of his colleague at work in Sedgeley Junction signal-box. The box closed in 1964 and was demolished after a fire had destroyed most of it. It was at the junction of the Dudley–Walsall line with the 'loop' up to Dudley Port High Level and also controlled the access to Palethorpes' Siding. (Cyril Hand.)

Signalman John James accepts the single-line token from the driver of the train that has just arrived from the Pensnett Branch at Kingswinford South Junction in class 47 diesel locomotive no. 47229, 10 September 1984. Note Signalman James is carrying the cloth that signalmen use when grabbing the levers in the box. The box itself is on the far right of the picture and controlled the junction of the Pensnett–Wombourn line with the GWR main West Midland line, as well as the sidings and yards on both sides of this line. (Ned Williams.)

From the windows of Oldbury (Bromford Lane) signal-box, Signalman Cyril Hand recorded the platelayers at work at the Birmingham end of Oldbury & Bromford Lane station – now the site of Sandwell & Dudley station – in about 1960. The far tracks went into the station's goods yard, and in the background is the Birmingham–Wolverhampton canal, the BCN. (Cyril Hand.)

Ganger Dan Brew, on his motorized platelayer's inspection trolley, June 1935. This was introduced on the Wombourn line on 8 January 1934 and was shedded at Tettenhall, although the length of track for which Dan Brew was responsible ran from near Penn Halt to Baggeridge Junction. (Collection of Peter Brew.)

Phyllis Rudd and 'Jack' at Willenhall (Stafford Street) LMS Goods Yard, 1942. Phyllis responded to wartime pleas for women to join the railway workforce. She left her job in a fruit shop hoping to become a railway guard but became a cart driver based in Willenhall. She was nineteen at the time, and, as a child, had been terrified of horses. (Collection of Phyllis Rudd.)

The last locomotive to be repaired at Stafford Road Works, Wolverhampton, leaves the premises, 11 February 1964. (The works closed officially on 1 June 1964.) Employees at the works lined up to say farewell to class 28xx, 2–8–0 no. 2859 on that grey morning. Men have passed away, and the works has been demolished, but the locomotive is now preserved and runs on the Severn Valley Railway! (Fred Richardson.)

Acknowledgements

I would like to express my thanks to the following people who have made photographs available:

Ralph Amos • George Bennett • Lawrence Brownhill • Paul Birchill
Black Country Society • Fred Braybrook • Peter Brew • the late W.A. Camwell
Roger Carpenter • Joe Challingsworth • Roger Crombleholme
Darlaston Local History Society • John Davenport • John Dew
Simon Dewey • Paul Dorney • Dianna Dors • John Dunn • Anne Gale
Norman Glover • Peter Green • Jack Haddock • L. Hanson • Peter Hale
Letitia Harris • Nigel Hazlewood • Industrial Railway Society
Johan Van Leerzem's Phil Lycett Collection • Michael Mensing • Viv Morgan
Ron Moss • Gordon Nutt • David Owen • Michael Paine • G. Parkes
Barry Price • Fred Richardson • Brian Robbins • Eric Rogers
the late Joe Russell • John Selway • Robert Selvey • Graham Sidwell
Ray Shill • the late Peter Shoesmith • Tim Shuttleworth • Roy Smith
Richard Taylor • David Wilson

BRITAIN IN OLD PHOTOGRAPHS

To order any of these titles please telephone Littlehampton Book Services on 01903 721596